Make This House Into A Home

Karen Seymore Portman

Make This House Into A Home
Copyright © 2012 by Karen Seymore Portman

P.O. Box 39 ~ Haymarket, VA 20168

First published in paperback 2012
Reprint edition 2015

All scriptures references are from New King James version
unless otherwise noted.

ISBN: 978-0-9964047-1-6

Dedication

My parents had favorite passages in the Bible that kept them through difficult times in their lives. My father has often stated that Psalm 121 kept him focused through many storms in his life and my mom often referenced and quoted Psalm 23, claiming the Lord to be her Shepherd. There were many times I would hear her singing Precious Lord.

We all need something positive to hang on to and both of theirs was the Word of God, which became mine too. Using the Word, I prayed for inner healing which meant change in my life. I pray that you, as the reader, will see the hope in this message and will also look to Jesus as your Help.

Therefore, this book is dedicated to everyone in need of inner healing in order to be all that God has created them to be so they can live life more abundantly, laugh more frequently, and love unconditionally!

Table of Contents

Introduction

AS I began writing this book, it became personal in a lot of ways. However, the one reason that stands out the most has to do with not only myself but the many individuals I run into almost daily who are crying inwardly. This book magnified my awareness of the emphasis we naturally put on the outward appearance versus the inward.

Early 2010 as I was looking over my life, I asked God to change some things about me. I remember He responded by saying, "OK. But you're not going to like it all." I wasn't expecting a reply like that. After all, how can we not like changes orchestrated by God? Well, let's just say adjustments started taking place immediately and it was on!

In the latter part of the summer of 2011, God began speaking to me about transformation. Then, I received the word metamorphosis while in prayer. I briefly studied the process a caterpillar goes through in order to become a butterfly. As a matter of fact, it's an egg first before becoming the larva, the caterpillar. Even after that, it becomes a pupa, a time when it's enclosed before the official unveiling. But the significant thing about that entire process is that in each phase a complete, recognizable change occurs. A change happens that does not look anything like the previous step but in the end, there emerges a beautiful butterfly with wings to fly.

Shortly after receiving that revelation and studying the key words transformation and metamorphosis, I listened to, "Show Me Your Ways," from Spirit Songs by Dr. Robin Harfouche with Christian Harfouche Ministries. Although the main parts of this song have been performed by other recording artists, it was this version that I listened to. It's almost forty minutes in length. About half-way through the song, the ministry team begins to sing prophetically. There was a section that caught my attention. I grabbed hold of those words that were sung after one of the leads expressed how she wanted to be used by God in many ways. The eye opening words were:

"I know I can't do it in my own strength
I know I don't know everything I need to know
But I'm gonna move my life around, Lord
And I'm gonna open every door to You my Savior
Walk into this house
Live in every room
Clean it out
Make me gold through and through
Polish me for You
And then let Your glory flow through me
Like a river from Heaven above"

I played just that portion repeatedly until it resonated deep within my spirit. The image that came to me was a room in a house that's either a storage room or not in the best condition at the moment to leave the door open if guests are around. Some of us can probably relate to an unexpected friend stopping by either announced or unannounced and not having our place looking completely to our liking. Those times will cause us to "close the door" so that if they pass by that particular room, they won't see the disarray inside.

The lyrics spoke of change. Change first by acknowledging that without God, we can't change. Then, make a decision to move things around in our lives in order for the change process to begin, so we can be completely used by God. The song continues with stating that every door will be opened to our house, our spiritual house, to welcome the Holy Spirit to freely live in us and make necessary changes. Why? So that His glory will flow through us.

This means, we become vulnerable in a good way. No more closed doors. No more being ashamed of a guest seeing our rooms. No more fear of change. It says, welcome Holy Spirit. We welcome Him in to clean us up. We welcome Him in to transform us. We welcome Him in to start the metamorphosis process on us.

If we don't change, nothing changes. Change is necessary in order to bring wholeness into every area of our lives. It starts with a personal cry to God. Even people who may appear to look like they "have it all" can be miserable on the inside. I'm convinced that I don't have *'nothing'* at all without Jesus.

My prayer is that this book will bring healing to individuals, marriages and families. Allow the metaphor of a house becoming a home warm your heart as it did mine. Then, let's allow God to do the surgery necessary on us to transform us into His image and resurrect us from dead situations by His resurrection power!

May God bless you and keep you in His perfect peace!

Karen Seymore Portman

You will keep in him in perfect peace, whose mind is stayed on You, because he trusts in You.
Isaiah 26:3

Information

I've always loved music. It's one of the ways God chooses to communicate with me. For the most part, I like various types of music except ones with degrading or negative lyrics. Music is a form of art. It's expressive. Oftentimes, but not always, one can tell what's really going on with an artist by the type of songs they sing or produce. Or for the listeners, by the type of songs they listen to, especially during certain seasons in their lives. At least I can say it's true for me.

When this piece was in its early stages of formation, two songs came to mind -- *A House is Not a Home* by the late recording artist, Luther Vandross and *Home* by Stephanie Mills. Although someone else could have recorded both songs, I remember these artists.

Some of the lyrics from Vandross' song states, *"A chair is still a chair, even when there's no one sitting there ... A room is still a room, even when there's nothin' there but gloom. But a room is not a house, and a house is not a home ...".* And, Mills' version of "Home" reflected on home as a place where love is overflowing; that longing to be in a place that is warm and safe.

11

I can truly say that several years ago those songs were just lovely songs with a soothing meaning; however, now, because I'm in a different place spiritually, they both have a new meaning. When I pondered over the lyrics from them, I closed my eyes and imagined what I thought the artists were saying. Since music is a form of expression, I allowed the lyrics to speak personally to me. The words really came alive after I watched the movie, *Are We Done Yet?* (Carr, 2007). Now, when I hear those songs, I see things that make a house different from a home.

If you've ever purchased a home, I think you would agree that it can be a lengthy process because you want to find just the right place when making a purchase of that magnitude. I know I did. It's not like going to buy a piece of clothing – it's an investment. You're actually looking for a place to call home.

I remember the first time I was looking for a house to call my home. Throughout the entire process, the realtor constantly reminded me of many things to consider, such as: location (or as she would say "location, location, location!"), public transportation, area schools, distance to/from work, the neighborhood conveniences, future development in the area/zoning, and many other things, some which I had not thought of. Oh, and let me say 'location' again! That was drilled into me. When I found what I believed to be that "perfect" place, I began to see it as home and that was different than looking for a house. It was something that felt right on the outside and on the inside.

12

I remember arriving at one location in a nice, quiet neighborhood. The house was on a slight incline but not much. It was just enough to be noticed on the corner. The landscaping was beautiful and according to the description, it had all the features I was looking for. When the realtor opened the door, the space inside was strikingly beautiful, even empty. I have to admit, I was impressed. I began to smell the fragrance of "home". It wasn't until we opened the basement door that a damp, musky smell hit our nostrils. We thought 'uh oh' but continued down the stairs.

We were expecting to see a flood since there had been several days of rain prior too but that wasn't the case. It wasn't until our feet hit the carpet that there was a squishy sound. The entire carpet was soaked but without the visible appearance of being soaked. It was obvious that there had been water damage from all the rain. The outside layer of the carpet showed no signs. That's because the damage was lying underneath the carpet and padding. Of course the damp odor was evident of something but it was only after we stepped on the carpet that we knew where the stench was coming from.

I'm not sure if the owner was aware since the house was vacant but of course, that cancelled my interest ... immediately. Before leaving the premises, we discovered a drainage problem in the stairwell as we walked around the outside. If it had not rained several days prior to or if it had not been discovered during inspection, I probably would have gone through the purchase process, and if successful, the problem would have surfaced later. This brings me to the movie.

Revelation

Moving will often force us to deal with those *beasts in the basement* even if we don't want to. Between the packing and cleaning, we stumble across old memories, some good and some bad. Either way, it causes us to reminisce. Because we are important to God, He's concerned about the things underneath our surface. It doesn't matter what our outward appearance looks like, God looks at our inward -- our heart (1 Sam 16:7).

> 7 But the Lord said to Samuel,"Do not look at his appearance or at his physical stature, because I have refused him. For the Lord does not see as man sees; for man looks at the outward appearance, but the Lord looks at the heart." 1 Sam 16:7

The first time I watched *Are We Done Yet?* I received a refreshing, spiritual revelation from a family entertainment movie. For the sake of those who have not watched the movie, allow me to summarize while sharing the revelation God gave to me.

The Decision

The movie opened showing the Persons' family living in a small condo in a busy city. It appeared the couple had recently gotten married and the father welcomed the role of being a dad to his wife's children. The condo was the perfect place for a bachelor; however, now being a husband with two children and a dog, they were obviously cramped, but they were adjusting. Then his wife announced that she was pregnant. That's when Nick, the husband, decided that the family had outgrown his bachelor pad in the city. It was time to move.

The couple set out to look for a new place to call home for their growing family. They found their dream house nestled in a quiet community, rich with nature and clean air. The house had everything the parents wanted. It was away from the noise of the city, the air was fresh, the landscaping was flawless, the neighbors were the perfect "welcome wagon", the outside and inside were gorgeous, the views were breathtaking, and the separate office space was perfect for Nick, the aspiring magazine writer. What more could a family want? Now they had to convince the children that moving away from their friends was the right thing to do.

The family met Chuck the town realtor among many other persons when the time was right. You'll read more about his ever changing roles. He really promoted the house on their walk-thru even though a few things "fell" off along the way. Chuck referred to those as minor repairs compared to what the Persons would be getting for their money. He even recommended a local contractor to fix those small items.

The staging could not have been more perfect. With very little persuasion, the parents were convinced that this house was an absolute steal they could afford. This would become the new home for their growing family. They moved in and the demolition derby began. Their lives changed forever ... but in good ways.

The Problems

Things hidden behind and under outward layers started to go wrong that were not visible during the walk-thru. Later in the movie, it became apparent that Chuck was well aware of the problems beforehand but purposely neglected to inform the Persons before they purchased it. The first problem started with a faulty electrical system. Nick called the contractor recommended by Chuck. When Chuck arrived as the contractor, Nick was surprised. He was not only the town realtor, but also the town contractor. Chuck wore another hat.

After inspecting the problem, Chuck informed Nick that it was larger than he thought and so was the price he quoted. Nick threw Chuck off the premises and decided to find a way to repair it himself ... cheaper. So, Nick hired an unlicensed contractor to do the electrical work at a bargain rate and that's just what he received – a bargain job.

With his chest stuck out for fixing the problem, Nick labeled Chuck as a crook. He was proud of his decision that saved the family thousands of dollars at the small cost of not being able to run a few common household appliances at the same time. He justified it by saying, 'anyone should know that.'

The next day Chuck showed up but this time as the City Inspector. Talk about a man with many hats! He cited Nick with a fine for tapping into the neighbor's power supply and he turned his power off. The quick, cheap fix ended up not being the lasting solution. After begging Chuck to put his contractor hat back on so he could negotiate a deal for the repairs, he did and the power was restored. But the problems didn't stop there. It was just the beginning.

Chuck ended up being the town's everything. Not only was he the town realtor, the contractor, and the city inspector, but he became the project manager over this major home renovation job. Every time something else was uncovered that needed repairing, Chuck brought a crew in to fix it and the cost of the house was starting to go up. Some of the damages included: a problem with raccoons, severe dry rot behind the walls, termite infestation under the floor boards, corroded water pipes under the house, and a rotted glass door frame, just to name a few.

Most homeowners are familiar with the term gutting out. Well, talk about being gutted out! Chuck told Nick it would get ugly before it got pretty, and that it did. The families dream house now ended up a total mess. It quickly went from picture perfect to a major fixer upper. It had to be totally renovated from the inside out. The house became unrecognizable as the movie continued.

The Repairs

It seemed like overnight, the peaceful quiet of being away from the city was being re-lived by the daily pounding, knocking and drilling done by different experts brought in to make the repairs. Nothing was in its original state when the house was purchased. Even the floors they walked across during the walk-thru were uprooted due to termite infestation.

As the crew tore the house apart, the owner began to think he had made a huge mistake. But Chuck, being the real estate agent, knew something about the house that the Persons didn't. He knew the real value. He didn't just see it as a house. He saw it as a home. A home that was fit for the Persons. Therefore, Chuck only saw it as just needing a little work. But he also knew that if he had revealed what he knew in the beginning to the family, they would have walked away from the house that was meant to be their home.

19

The length of time to repair all the hidden damages began to grow and Chuck, as the project manager, moved on premises in his trailer to keep a close watch on the project. At least that was his excuse at the time. The original purchase price of the house, that once was a steal, had now gone up tremendously. It was no longer looking like a bargain to Nick. In order for the team to fix everything that needed repairing, they had to go under the surface to fix the real problem. None of the jobs they tackled were easy.

We know a house is only as strong as its foundation. So for Nick, the last straw came when Chuck delivered the news during child birth classes, a time when both parents should be peaceful and calm, that the house needed a whole new foundation. Chuck had a way of sneaking in the most horrific news to Nick. Nick exploded! Chuck quickly tried to divert Nick's attention back to the unborn babies so they wouldn't get upset. What a blow. That was it! To hear that news must have devastated Nick. Now, with a 'wrecking crew' on the premises and the house completely dismantled, Nick fired Chuck and decided to fix the house himself.

Chuck was sad because Nick was so upset with him. He confessed that he knew about the repairs before selling them the house. With his realtor hat back on, he explained to Nick that he also knew the value of the property. He knew the costs of repairs were far less than what the place would become to the Persons – a home. Chuck knew that if Nick had focused on the cost of the repairs that needed to be done, he would have missed seeing the value of the house that, with a few repairs, would become their home.

Nick's ears were closed to excuses. He blamed Chuck for everything which took me back to the scene in the Garden of Eden in the Bible in Genesis 3:11-13. It seems like the blame game continues today. Yet, still trying, Chuck put on another hat and offered his services as a licensed couple's therapist to restore their relationship.

Nick was furious! He refused this offer and yelled, "Get out!" As Chuck sadly departed, his words to Nick were, "If you can't see the value of a home as opposed to a house, then maybe I'm not your guy." He left and because of the loyalty of the other working crew to Chuck, they left too.

The Home

Time passed and Nick began repairing the home by himself. His wife and children had moved into the guest house on the premises and he found himself all alone. Then something happened that caused Nick to see life differently. It was during this time that a neighbor told Nick that Chuck's wife was not overseas on tour as he had previously stated; she had died in a tragic accident. This revealed why Chuck was so passionate about making the Persons' house a home.

Even though Chuck had a home, after the passing of his wife, it became a house. He locked up his house and stayed in a mobile home parked in his yard. Being around the Persons and other people reminded him of the home he once had. The loss of his wife emptied his house and ultimately, his life. The smell of home was no longer in the air. No one was there for him to turn the key and find there saying she was still in love with him. His joy was taken and he died along with his wife. That's probably why he busied himself working so many jobs. It kept his mind off of facing realty and dealing with his own pain. Even though Chuck was busy trying to help the Persons, his own need for healing was revealed. It was obvious he had a broken heart.

Chuck understood the value of a home from two perspectives. The first was having loved ones around to share special times with, and the second, beauty on the outside is only as good as beauty on the inside. The Persons reminded Chuck of the home he once had. They gave him life and hope in a situation that had died for him.

To fast forward, Nick went to visit Chuck and their broken relationship was restored. Nick finally understood what Chuck was trying to get him to see all along. Nick returned home to finish the repairs. Shortly after returning home, Chuck was called to wear another hat but this time as a midwife to deliver the Persons' twins. This scene contributed to the healing that Chuck needed.

When he received the call, he needed something from inside his house he had locked up in order to help the Persons. Chuck had to face his own fears before he could assist the family. And he did. The movie ended with the birth of the twins and Chuck and the team of experts returning to complete the home repairs. The house became a home and Nick had a new meaning of value.

Truth Revealed

What a revelation for me! It's amazing how a family comedy was used to open my eyes and bring revelation to God's truth. Wow! Think about it in terms of the way God sees us. He knows our value. He knows of the things lying underneath our surface that clothes and make-up cannot hide that are in need of fixing. He doesn't care how long the process takes. He just wants us to deal with it so we can be whole. Afterwards, I was able to connect that to a real situation that happened with a friend. Even though this is one example I'm using, I'm sure it fits the picture of many people we run into.

It happened during a personal visit with a friend in a very dark place in her life. In order to maintain the confidentiality, I'll use the name Hurting to represent my friend. Hurting was battling with depression due to sudden losses and changes in her life; therefore, I decided to go over and cook a hot meal to cheer her up. I was taught from childhood to always call before stopping by someone's house but this particular day, I didn't do it. I knew from previous attempts that if I called first, Hurting would talk me out of coming. So I decided to surprise her. I didn't want to bring a pre-prepared meal; one can get those anytime. I wanted to prepare a hot one while on the premises and I was hoping to enjoy it with good conversation. After all, I had known Hurting a long time.

It was just approaching evening and I was feeling pretty good when I arrived at the house. Notice I said 'house'. I rang the doorbell and to my surprise, Hurting was still in bed and had been that way all day. I entered with grocery bags in my hands and joy in my heart but soon felt the weight of oppression in the atmosphere. The thought I once had of cheering up a long-time friend became quite the opposite. No matter what I did to try to change the mood, my joy was slowly fading due to the heaviness around me.

The house was dark and cold. Not only because the curtains were still pulled, but because there was gloominess all around. The surroundings depressed me. There were no smells of home in the air. Everything around me was screaming, *"Depressed, depressed – can someone please numb my pain!"* The house was a dwelling place but not a home. Although furnishings were neatly in place, the house didn't feel anything like what a home should represent.

This took me back to the lyrics in Luther Vandross' song, A House Is Not A Home, *"A chair is still a chair even when there's no one sitting there. A room is still a room, even when there's nothin' there but gloom. But a room is not a house and a house is not a home ...".* The furnishings were in position, the rooms formed the house but the smells of home and the people who make a home special were missing when "the key was turned," or in my case, when she opened the door.

The weight of oppression was draining my spirit. It's something about God's light that will cause darkness to become more noticeable. Once exposed to brightness, we recognize when the lights are out or it's dim. I sensed Hurting had been in the bed all day surrounded by torment and depression and didn't know it, so I decided to tough it out, still wanting to make the evening special. I chose to continue on with the original plan even though I was told I could leave.

Hurting told me she was not hungry but I fired up the stove anyway. She went back to her room and I continued preparing the meal. As the aroma of a few of her favorite foods began to fill the house ... steamed cabbage with a hint of garlic, potatoes with onions, fried fish and cornbread, and the heat from the stove began to warm the atmosphere, something changed. Hurting came out of the room and said, "I didn't think I was hungry but now you've made me hungry. How much longer? When will the food be ready?" All of sudden, the food couldn't cook fast enough. I was rushed to get it on the table. The smell of home began to intoxicate her. There was an atmospheric change from something as simple as a home cooked meal. What a shift change in Hurting's mood!

This dark and lonely place could happen to any of us if we allow our circumstances to dictate our atmosphere. We have to be careful of things that cause us to draw our curtains. Closed curtains keep the light out and box us in. There is a voice on the inside screaming, "Can anyone see that I'm hurting and want out of here?" Without being around loving people or being actively engaged in positive activities to warm our hearts, we stop living.

Dark clouds of depression form over us and hold our minds and thoughts captive. We lock our own selves up as prisoners. We focus on what we don't have and what could of-should have been instead of allowing God's fragrance to permeate our minds and change the atmosphere in our rooms. Once our mind is filled with negative thoughts, they become a part of our heart, and out of our heart, we begin to speak it and then we believe it. Then our words begin to shape our life and every person and thing around us (Luke 6:45).

> *A good man out of the good treasure of his heart brings forth good; and an evil man out of the evil treasure of his heart brings forth evil. For out of the abundance of the heart his mouth speaks. Luke 6:45*

But there is good news. We can decide to let the light in or continue to sit in darkness. If we allow the light of Jesus in, His sweet fragrance will fill us. Then, we too will come out and say, "I'm hungry". We'll be fed by God's Word. Our thirst will be quenched and He will take us through the process so that our house can become a home too.

Application

Revelation should bring us to application. It is truth revealed put into action. We should now ask the question, "How can I apply this lesson to bring change to my current situation?"

Once again, this took me back to the two songs. Even though I knew the lyrics from *back in the day,* I wanted to make sure I didn't overlook any words so I looked them up on the internet to make sure I had them both correct. The words came alive to me! They took on a new meaning from when I remembered them before. I believe that it's largely due to my spiritual walk now.

God revealed it to me this way: Rooms are separators and furnishings are things but they can't make a home. There are two scenarios that came to mind. The first one is of a person who grew up in a loving environment but now find himself or herself in a new land or perhaps things have changed in their lives, causing what they once viewed as normal to now be abnormal. The second is of a person who never knew real love because they never felt

28

that they were loved, even though, or perhaps not, they knew it was possible. In either case, a home should represent that place of warmth, acceptance, and love.

We may recognize that the way things are is not the norm and God wants to fix that. God wants to be the Contractor of our minds and hearts. He can take a major fixer-upper and restore it better than the original with all new upgrades. New upgrades in the way we think. New upgrades in the way we see life. New upgrades in the way we love.

Once I got that revelation, I began to chase God for the application. I wanted to know how to apply that in my own life spiritually. Sometimes that's the hardest hurdle because it causes us to uncover pain lying beneath the surface. It causes us to open some boxes we tucked away in that unused space. It forces us to clean our house! As we work through the process of transformation, we begin to see others through the eyes of Jesus. We see their pain hiding behind their outward appearance and we want them to experience the same transformation.

Just like the realtor in the movie understood the value of the house with some work to turn it into a home, God knows the value of us (Psalm 139). He's aware of the work that's needed to make us whole and what's required in order to be that place where He can dwell freely. I believe this is a lifetime process because we should always be growing in Him daily.

Our outward appearance can say many things but what's underneath may be dry rotted or eaten up by termites. In order to deal with them, we have to allow God to have full access without holding anything back. In the Introduction I shared the lyrics from the prophetic version of "Show Me Your Way". In order to have the Spirit live freely in every room, we need to freely open up the doors.

> 12 For the word of God is living and powerful, and sharper than any two-edged sword, piercing even to the division of soul and spirit, and of joints and marrow, and is a discerner of the thoughts and intents of the heart. 13 And there is no creature hidden from His sight, but all things are naked and open to the eyes of Him to whom we must give account.
> Hebrews 4:12-13

God loves us. God loves family. God loves marriages. God loves children. God loves healthy relationships. God is love. However, His love will sometimes require us to go into His operating room and under His knife. The knife is His Word – the sword of the Spirit (Hebrews 4:12-13). Knowing what the Word says sets us free. Nick thought he could do the repairs himself but spiritually speaking, we know that we can't do anything apart from Christ (John 8:32 and John 15:5).

In the movie, the house became a total wreck before it was transformed into a beautiful home. That can happen to us. Sometimes things appear to get worse before they get better but, if we hang in there, there is light after all the debris is cleaned up.

> *32 And you shall know the truth, and the truth shall make you free."*
> *John 8:32*
>
> *5 "I am the vine, you are the branches. He who abides in Me, and I in him, bears much fruit; for without Me you can do nothing. John 15:5*

At the end of the movie, the Persons, Chuck, the contractors, and the entire community got that. Joy was restored for all! There was help for them and there is help for us. When we don't get it, there are those that will come alongside us to help bring light into our darkness. They know by God's revelation what's really going on inside.

If we're busy adorning the outside it's hard to see the inside. In our own eyes and perhaps in the eyes of some people, we look good. However, when we allow the Holy Spirit to take up residence in us, it's hard to stay the same. A metamorphosis takes place and we begin to transform (Romans 12:2). The old stuff is ripped up. It's that stuff that's been in our family line or in our mindset for years, old behavior patterns and anything else that can affect who we are. A shift happens

> *2 And do not be conformed to this world, but be transformed by the renewing of your mind, that you may prove what is that good and acceptable and perfect will of God. Romans 12:2*

in our environment.   An honest inventory leads to an honest assessment.

We're healed when we can be naked and unashamed; unashamed and transparent about the things that held us captive because we've been renovated by the Holy Spirit. Chuck stated in the movie, *'with dry rot you never know how bad it is until you get into it.'* We can take that to be a revelation when truth is revealed. We never know how bad it is until we look into it.

After God renovates us or as He's doing the work within us, we are in a better position to see others crying inside too. We see the internal war going on. For those not in a relationship with Christ, we begin to see the natural and spiritual deaths. And just like Chuck who also needed his own healing, it becomes hard for us to sit back and do nothing. God wants to restore us so we're healed from the inside out.   It was a process for the Persons' home renovation, and it's a process for us.

Now, when I hear either song, I visualize something special – something very peaceful. The song "Home" recorded by Stephanie Mills was originally performed as part of the Broadway Musical, *The Wiz*, an adaptation of the classic, *The Wonderful Wizard of Oz*. In *The Wiz*, Dorothy was taken from a place of love, comfort and protection and thrust into a strange land as a result of a storm – a twister. That abrupt change disrupted her life; however, while in her fantasy world, she learned friendship and love. In Vandross' song, *"A House is Not a Home"*, he wanted to turn the key and find that special person in his life inside, still in love with him. The furnishings and rooms were not important without the person there whom he loved present to share it with.

In both songs, although the circumstances were different, they both longed to feel the love and affection that a home should have. Turning to God, Mills' asked, *"If you're listening God, please don't make this hard."* That's what we long for. We long for an easy process to work out the issues in order to bring a fantasy world of love into reality. In other words, if I allow God to take me through the process His way, I pray that He will make it easy by renovating me gently but get the job done.

When a house is up for sale, it was just that – a house. But we need it to say home for us. We want to feel relaxed when inside. We desire to have the smell of peace. We want Christ's aroma to permeate the air. Even staged homes, as beautiful as they are to entice us to purchase, are still not ours until we personalize them to our liking. Our personal warmth and touch make it uniquely ours.

I remember choosing the paint for my home and the painter said, "Don't look at what the previous owner had; think about what you like because you have to live with it." So like a home, when we accept Christ, we become His dwelling place and He adds His personal touch to us. He treats us each individually and that's what makes us unique.

The Word of God is like that. We have to take His Word and personalize it for us, because it's for us. The Word does not change but we do. True beauty outside is a result of real beauty inside. When the house was re-paired, all those things that had rotted on the inside became brand new.

Transformation

Although the movie was very comical and many points were apparent, four things became very clear to me:

1. The house was occupied before the clean up began.
2. The damage underneath the exterior surfaces were exposed and had to be dealt with.
3. The owner had to agree to the costs and the lengthy repairs to be done by a team of experts.
4. The house finally became a home.

These points made me think about our relationship with God through Jesus Christ, our Savior:

1. The Holy Spirit must take up residence in us before the clean up can begin.
2. The Holy Spirit reveals damaged areas in our life in order to bring healing and restoration.
3. The Holy Spirit is our Expert and works with us through the process, no matter how long it takes at

no cost. The price was already paid on the cross at Calvary.
4. The glory of God is revealed in us from the inside out.

When we accept Christ as our Lord and Savior, we invite the Holy Spirit to move in and reside in us. We become new creatures. A spiritual transformation happens and anything that's below the surface will be dealt with over time. It's not meant to torment us; it's meant to bring healing and restoration so we can begin to move forward towards our destiny.

God is the Project Manager and He gently removes the old foundation and builds a new foundation on His Word. That foundation will be solid. Because of His love, we won't look like a total mess in front of others as He's working on us like the dismantled house in the movie. God is not out to humiliate us. He just wants to help us. The result, people will begin to see the change as He ever so gently unwrap us. Our outward appearance will be a result of our inward change if we allow Him to transform us. Even though

And we know that all things work together for good to those who love God, to those who are the called according to His purpose. Romans 8:28

the situation may appear to look worse, in our eyes, He's working it out for our good according to Romans 8:28.

We shouldn't worry about what others think as we're going through the transformation process. It's something about being naked and unashamed that just feels good. If we're not willing to change, we will never fully launch into the things that God created us to do.

Sometimes others can see God's potential in us before we can. That's why during this process He may send others our way to give us the nudge we need. I'm convinced that people are sent our way to help take the spiritual blinders off, just like Chuck was sent to the Persons. But we have to be willing to let go of our security blankets holding our fears.

A Personal Decision

Dealing with truth without the use of photo touch-up software is hard. The Persons' dream house turned into a nightmare. I'm sure they thought there was no way out. Looking at piles of rubbish can be depressing within itself whether self inflicted or from circumstances beyond our control. But if we don't discard the rubbish in the proper disposal places, it can become a breeding place for many uninvited "guests". Like Hurting, we'll no longer open our curtains. We'll stay in bed, and simply stop living.

But God knew that hurts would come upon us. He knew it was necessary to restore the relationship of fallen man back unto Him. That's why *Isaiah 61* is one of the scriptures foretelling the Good News of Salvation, Jesus the Christ, our Savior. The One that was sent to protect, preserve, deliver, and redeem us. In the first verse, it says, "... He has sent Me to heal the brokenhearted, to proclaim liberty to the captives, and the opening of the prison to those who are bound ...". Jesus restored our relationship back to the Father. The Word of God says, if we cry out to Him, He will hear us and help us as stated in Psalm 34:17.

> The righteous cry out, and the LORD hears, and delivers them out of all their troubles. Psalm 34:17

Just because we find ourselves in one state does not mean we have to stay that way. The process of inner healing can sometimes take years; however, I've come to realize that it's not how we start something, it's how we finish. The shortest way is not always the best way. It's a process but He is our qualified Expert. His way may not be the shortest route or the most appealing to us; however, if we stay on the path directed by Him, we'll get to our destination and learn some things along the way. During the process our faith will be increased and a deeper level of trust will be established.

Think about it in terms of taking a trip. Sometimes taking the interstate may be the fastest way, especially if we are traveling between several states. We can travel at a higher rate of speed; we have access to more lanes to maneuver around the slower traffic; there are more oppor-tunities to pull off for rest breaks; and, we get there faster but with a little less scenery of the cities and towns we are travelling through.

However, there will be times when God will take us the scenic route where the speed limit will be slower, we will find ourselves behind slower moving vehicles with no pass-ing allowed, and more time will be added to our trip. He just might have us stop along the way to capture a scenic view, pick up blessings, learn life lessons, or to meet people. We'll eventually reach our destination knowing God's hand guided us all the way. We'll have a new level of faith because we've learned to depend on God. We'll learn to trust and obey hearing His voice for direction. We'll be fueled with courage. We'll lean on Him as we're faced with other challenges. We'll understand that what we thought was a setback in our eyes was actually a set up with God.

By the time the movie ended, everyone had learned something. The blended family bonded. Nick became aware of the driving force behind Chuck's passion for a home. Chuck faced his fear and went into his house in or-der to help someone else. The people in the town became a family. Forgiveness and reconciliation occurred. And last but certainly not least, the house finally became a home for the Persons.

A Final Thought

I've had many personal encounters with God since I began my journey with Him several years ago. I remember one in particular that happened in 2007 as I was washing dishes. I began to cry out to God about a lot of things going on in my life and I desired to be free. It was at that moment that I suddenly stopped washing dishes and found myself stretched out, prostrate on my living room floor. I continued crying to God and suddenly, I saw a vision of a very long sharp object, sticking from my front stomach area where my spirit man is. I recognized it when I saw it. It represented every person and everything that caused pain in my life and it was still there.

God began to speak to me. He let me know that it had been there for a long time and that I was afraid to remove it because if I took it out, the place where it had been lodged for so long would begin to bleed. However, He said the blood is where the healing begins. He reminded me of what took place on the cross for me. He said removing it will leave a scar but only as evidence of His resurrection power that healed me. It reminded me when Thomas needed to see the nail print in Jesus' hands in John 20:24-29 in order to believe that it was actually Christ who had risen.

After receiving such revelation, I got up from the floor, excited that God had revealed my wounds and this fear to me. I praised God, continued my chores and later dressed for church. After service was over, my pastor prayed for me. Not knowing about my earlier encounter with God, he said, "I see something sticking in you," and he pulled it out in the spirit. How strange, I thought. That was revealed at home and I had praised God over the revelation.

When I returned home, I asked God what happened. I wanted to know why it was still there. He responded, "Even though I showed it to you and you got so excited over the revelation, you never removed it." Wow! What a revelation and I had to chuckle over it. God is about bringing things to completion if we allow Him. Because I had cried out to be free, He heard me and started the job as my Personal Contractor and Personal Trainer. I'm thankful today that He continues to hear my cries and always respond. He will complete His work in me.

> ... *being confident of this very thing, that He who has begun a good work in you will complete it until the day of Jesus Christ;*
> *Philippians 1:6*

Salvation

S alvation is deliverance. I shared all of this to say, if you will allow God to do it, He will also reveal and remove the things that's sticking in you or buried underneath the surface so that you can be free. Even as He showed it to me and I thought it was over, He let me know that I didn't remove it after it was revealed. Once it was removed, spiritually, I felt different and the process of inner healing truly began. God values each of us. That's why He offered His only Son, Jesus Christ at a high price but our salvation is free. The price was already paid by the blood of Jesus. The cost of real love is without charge and it is priceless!

Do you want to feel different today? Do you want the love and warmth of a home versus a house? Do you want to allow God to move in and have complete access to every room in your house and change it into a home? If so, then I invite you to say the Prayer of Salvation. Once you've said the prayer, I encourage you, if you don't have a place to grow in your relationship with God, to find a place where you can be nurtured in His Word.

42

Prayer of Salvation

Lord, according to Romans 10:9, You said that if we
confess the Lord Jesus and believe in our hearts that God
raised Jesus from the dead, we shall be saved.
So right now, I confess that Jesus is Lord. I believe in my
heart that God raised Jesus from the dead. I accept Jesus
Christ as my personal Savior and according to Your word,
I am now saved.

*8 But what does it say? "The word is near you, in your mouth and in
your heart" (that is, the word of faith which we preach): 9 that if you
confess with your mouth the Lord Jesus and believe in your heart that
God has raised Him from the dead, you will be saved. 10 For with the
heart one believes unto righteousness, and with the mouth confession is
made unto salvation. 11 For the Scripture says, "Whoever believes on
Him will not be put to shame."   12 For there is no distinction between
Jew and Greek, for the same Lord over all is rich to all who call upon
Him. 13 For "whoever calls on the name of the Lord shall be saved."*
Romans 10:8-13

The following is The Resume of Jesus Christ, the author unknown.

The Resume of Jesus Christ
Address: Ephesians 1:20
Phone: Romans 10:13
Website: The Bible . Keywords: Christ, Lord, Savior and Jesus

Objective

My name is Jesus -The Christ. Many call me Lord! I've sent you my resume because I'm seeking the top management position in your heart. Please consider my accomplishments as set forth in my resume.

Qualifications

- I founded the earth and established the heavens (see Proverbs 3:19)
- I formed man from the dust of the ground (see Genesis 2:7)
- I breathed into man the breath of life (see Genesis 2:7)
- I redeemed man from the curse of the law (see Galatians 3:13)
- The blessings of the Abrahamic Covenant comes upon your life through me (see Galatians 3:14)

Occupational Background

- I've only had one employer (see Luke 2:49).
- I've never been tardy, absent, disobedient, slothful or disrespectful.
- My employer has nothing but rave reviews for me (see Matthew 3:15 -17)

Skills Work Experiences

Some of my skills and work experiences include: empowering the poor to be poor no more, healing the brokenhearted, setting the captives free, healing the sick, restoring sight to the blind and setting at liberty them that are bruised (see Luke 4:18).

I am a Wonderful Counselor (see Isaiah 9:6). People who listen to me shall dwell safely and shall not fear evil, (see Proverbs 1:33).

Most importantly, I have the authority, ability and power to cleanse you of your sins (see I John 1:7-9)

Educational Background

- I encompass the entire breadth and length of knowledge, wisdom and understanding (see Proverbs 2:6).
- In me are hid all of the treasures of wisdom and knowledge (see Colossians 2:3).
- My Word is so powerful; it has been described as being a lamp unto your feet and a light unto your path (see Psalm 119:105).
- I can even tell you all of the secrets of your heart, (see Psalm 44:21).

Major Accomplishments

- I was an active participant in the greatest Summit Meeting of all times, (See Genesis 1:26).
- I laid down my life so that you may live, (See II Corinthians 5:15).
- I defeated the arch enemy of God and mankind and made a show of them openly, (See Colossians 2:15).
- I've miraculously fed the poor, healed the sick and raised the dead!
- There are many more major accomplishments, too many to mention here. You can read them on my website, which is located at: www dot - the BIBLE. You don't need an Internet connection or computer to access my website.

References

Believers and followers worldwide will testify to my divine healing, salvation, deliverance, miracles, restoration and supernatural guidance.

In Summation

Now that you've read my resume, I'm confident that I'm the only candidate uniquely qualified to fill this vital position in your heart. In summation, I will properly direct your paths (see Proverbs 3:5-6), and lead you into everlasting life (see John 6:47). When can I start? Time is of the essence (see Hebrews 3:15).

Send this resume to everyone you know.
You never know who may have an opening!
Thanks for your help.

Author unknown

Works Cited

"Are We Done Yet?". Dir. Steve Carr. Perf. Ice Cube, Nia Long, John C McGinley, Aleisha Allen, and Philip Daniel Bolden. Sony Pictures. 2007. DVD.

Luther Vandross. "A House Is Not A Home." *Album title unknown.* Written by *unknown*. n.d., CD.

Dr. Robin Harfouche. "Show Me Your Ways." *Spirit Songs.* Written by *unknown*. CD.

Stephanie Mills. "Home." *Home.* Written by Charlie Smalls. 1989. CD.

About the Author

Karen Seymore Portman is a highly sought-after mentor, coach, seminar presenter, and teacher, and handles it all with humility. It only takes one encounter with Karen to realize she is gifted and anointed to do the work God has assigned to her hands. Her unquenchable desire to serve and her boundless energy makes her a formidable talent to harness. She equips equippers.

She plants intercessory prayer ministries; conducts various workshops on emotional healing, vision and purpose, prayer, women's issues, and a variety of other topics; teaches all generations; assists with revivals; and teaches all levels of prophetic classes for a virtual global school.

Karen operates in many spiritual gifts, teaching is but one of them. Her creativity in teaching classes is cleaver, vibrant, and delightful. The mark of a great teacher is that students seek them. She employs an unusual teaching style of first teaching a basic concept then immediately requiring students to demonstrate how the information is applied.

With a deep compassion to see people saved and fulfilling their destiny promised by God, Karen is driven to reach the lost, minister to individuals, and encourage people of all ages to walk in their purpose created by God.

This explains her call scripture in 2004, Isaiah 61:1-3 – *'to preach the gospel and to heal the brokenhearted'*. Although that's just one of her many favorite scriptures, as she continues to avail herself to the Lord, the one that could best represent her is found in Isaiah 6:8 -- ***Also I heard the voice of the Lord, saying: " Whom shall I send, and who will go for Us?" Then I said, "Here am I! Send me."***

www.ingramcontent.com/pod-product-compliance
Lightning Source LLC
Chambersburg PA
CBHW072040060426
42449CB00010BA/2361